I0173250

# 12 Lessons of Healing Through Grief

Cherie L. Barnes

GWW
PUBLISHING CO.

Published by
Greater Working Women Publishing, LLC
www.gwwpublishing.com

GWW
PUBLISHING CO.

Providing Publishing Services for Christian Authors & Organizations:
Hardbacks, Paperbacks, E-Books & Audiobooks.

12 Lessons of Healing Through Grief

Copyright © 2018 Cherie L. Barnes

All rights reserved. Printed in the United States of America. No part of this
book may be used or reproduced in any manner whatsoever without written
permission except in the case of brief quotations em-bodied in critical articles or
reviews.

ISBN: 978-1-948829-01-4

Second Edition: April 2018

10 9 8 7 6 5 4 3 2 1

## Dedication

This book is dedicated to all who have lost a loved one.
May your heart be comforted as you move toward
positive motions and actions in life.

# TABLE OF CONTENTS

# Acknowledgements

I am indebted to the following people for their love, support and help: To my mother and stepfather, Flecy and George for walking down this path with me, and my daughter, Nia who let mommy write at night.

To my family, extended family, friends, church family, and colleagues. Thank you, thank you, and thank you for being there for me.

To my Sister-in-Christ, Chantea M. Williams for giving me this arena to share my story. I am thankful for you in more ways than you know.

To Drs. Carol Collum and Sonia Kennedy for believing in me and sharing your wisdom with me.

To Virginia Johnson for taking my phone call many, many months ago to share with me what you know. What you shared with me has been invaluable.

To Greater Working Women Publishing Co. for this platform and this ministry.

And my Heavenly Father, I'm nothing without you!

# INTRODUCTION

This is more than a book! It is a guide to healing and hope. In the pages of this manuscript, you will find valuable information as it relates to the grieving and mourning process. These are lessons that I have learned along the way of life and wanted to share them with you. This has not been an easy process, but nevertheless, I have learned that you will get through the difficult hardships. Take notes, observe your own experiences, and consider how this book will enlighten you and share it with others. May the lessons I have learned along the way help you find comfort.

Blessings,
Cherie

# LESSON 1:

---

## GRIEVING IS NORMAL

Grief is the feeling of sorrow, sadness and deep mental anguish over the loss of a loved one. My experiences with grief over the years have been varied. I have noticed that with each person I have grieved, it has affected me in different ways. From the loss of my father to classmates to friends and to my significant other, my grief has lead me down a different pathway. I have learned valuable lessons and gained something different with each loss. Grieving is a normal process of life, although no one wants to be in this space. Each and everyone one of us has a different way of dealing and going through the grief process

Not everyone grieves and mourns the same way. Some people choose to keep quiet, while and others outwardly mourn. People will share with you different things in regards to what has worked for them or other experiences but it's important for you to find your new normal and remember the memories in your own way. You may have to remind people to respect your grieving process. Don't allow them to force you to do something that you're not comfortable doing.

At times it may not be possible to find a new normal right after your loss. Why? You are so use to having them in your life and nothing is the same now that they are gone. It can be difficult just getting out of bed. You may ask yourself the following questions:

- *How do I continue to live a "normal life"?*
- *Does anyone else feel the same way?*
- *How do I continue to move towards my goals and dreams?*
- *Who do I share my accomplishments with?*
- *Will it ever get any better?*
- *Will I ever be happy again?*

This is all part of the grieving process. Take it one day at a time. Don't rush your healing process. Don't apologize for your grief. Be intentional about surrounding yourself with people who love you and will support you. This is not something you should do alone. Allow people to be there for you just like you would for them.

# LESSON 2:

## GRIEVING IS RELEVANT

Taking time to grieve is a healing process. Extreme sadness leads to depression, somatic symptoms, loss of interest and withdrawal from family and friends. You lose the desire to be with people who matter and care about you. The depression may cause you to act and think like a different person. Someone that your family and friend do not recognize. If you have a family and others who depend on you, it is imperative that you do grieve, so that you can be available to them and meet their needs.

A friend of mine said to me that she puts her grief on the shelf and leaves it there. Wow! This is so profound and powerful. When she is ready, she will grieve in her own terms and in her own time frame. I can appreciate where she is coming from because I have done the same thing before. Some days grief is unbearable and other days it is tolerable.

Countless times during this ongoing process, I have allowed myself to think back to the day my life changed. It is painful to recall, in addition to, the associated memories.

Thinking back to where I was months ago, I would have done things differently. Do I regret some of the things that I have done, yes, but they were there to help and teach me a lesson that I needed to learn.

Grieving can be a very hard process and it is often more difficult when you are entrenched in it. I was given two books, *"Understanding Your Grief"* by Alan Wolfelt, PhD and *"I Wasn't Ready to Say Goodbye: Surviving, Coping and Healing after a Sudden Loss"* by Brook Noel and Pamela Blair, PhD. These two books have been so very enlightening. During this time, I learned about the term, "secondary losses", which are losses that occur in addition to the physical loss of the loved one. A secondary loss would be the loss of protection, security or other role(s) the deceased person played in a grieving person's life. These losses are sometimes just a dramatic as the initial loss of the loved one.

# LESSON: 3

# IT TAKES TIME

People have said to me, "You're not alright yet?" "You will be just fine. It takes a little time." I am now many months into my grieving process and yes, it is still hard! I am healing because I no longer wake up crying constantly as I did in the beginning.

In my other experiences with grief, I have learned that as each day passes, it is a different day. There are times I have felt that I should be okay, but as I have been told, it does take time. Grief does not stop or change overnight because it is a process. "Time heals all wounds," is something I have heard all my life when someone passes away.

There is no magic crystal ball that calculates when someone should be done with the crying, the mourning, the silence and the wondering thoughts of their loved one. Time waits for no one and time will pass you by if you let it. Do not stop and stand still in the process, allow time to be your friend and continue to move forward.

# LESSON: 4

---

# YOU NEED A SUPPORT SYSTEM

When you're grieving, you need someone to help you get through it. Somebody who is available to assist you in chores, childcare or sit with you is therapeutic. What you need the most is family, friends and colleagues to help you get through the rough times.

Everything done for and with the grieving person is appreciated, even if it is not acknowledged right away, forgotten or never. Know that their heart is full and very appreciative of the acts of kindness for them, from the initial moments of the loss, until the three to six months of the loss, ultimately until they are in a better place.

In my own experience, I have learned that I have the best support system in the world surrounding me. I cannot tell you how appreciative that I am and in indebted for my cheerleaders and support system. I have friends who got on airplanes, who drove many, many miles to see me and countless friends who still check on me.

My family has also been in my corner during this process and I cannot say thank you enough for all that you have done for me. If it was not for your help, I am not sure where I would be. My appreciation runs very deep. Thank you to my family and friends for sharing yourselves with me and being in this corner for me.

# LESSON: 5

## PRACTICE SELF-CARE

As a therapist and clinician, self-care is of utmost importance because it helps you heal. We tell our clients that this should be a regular practice, yet it is hard to take the same advice. In my time of grieving, I have not practiced self-care.

Grieving can be overwhelming sometimes with trying to adjust to a new normal, and self-care doesn't always seem to fit. Mediating for 1 to 2 minutes or taking 2-5 minutes alone in order do some deep breathing, can really make a difference. will enable you to heal should be why you are expending energy.

# LESSON: 6

## SEEK A HIGHER POWER

As a Christian going through this personal journey, I have had to rely on my faith and support of church family to help me get through this hard time in my life. I can remember the advice I received early on in my grieving from my Pastor and First Lady. I was looking for answers as to why my life was taking this turn.

I felt my life was in a very good place and now it was forever altered in a blink of an eye. The words I remember were, "Cherie, come to church even if you don't feel like it, because the more you come to church, the more word will get into you." I remember these words like it was yesterday! I still live by these words because there are times in which I do not want to attend church or bible study, because I am feeling low or discouraged.

I know each time I come to the house of the Lord, I am seeking the face of God and I want to be in His presence. As I am in His presence, I feel good and I do not want to leave. I would encourage anyone who is grieving to go to God. Talk to Him, read the Bible and tell Him how you are feeling. He listens to all our prayers and will not let you down. You must trust in Him and be surrounded in His love for true healing to happen.

# LESSON: 7

# FIND A HOBBY

Writing has been very beneficial for me. I can write to my heart's content, while getting lost in words and mediating on what I am thinking, feeling and experiencing. Reading has helped me tremendously. Picking up the Bible or other books, magazines, and listening to audio books or podcasts has put my mind at ease when I am anxious. I also love to cook and I find myself cooking food because it lifts my mood.

You can find yourself in the valley of life and emotions, but doing things that you find enjoyment in, certainly helps the healing process. Don't be afraid to start something new or pick up that hobby that you laid down. Now is the perfect time. You never know how a hobby can you help you put pieces of your life back together. It's all about surrounding yourself with positive activities. Things that can help bring a smile to your face. You may now feel like doing it every day but the days you do, enjoy it to the fullest.

# LESSON: 8

## IT'S OKAY TO CRY

Somedays you are fine with letting the tears bear themselves in your life and other times you want to cry, but no tears will come out. Crying is cleansing and needed to move forward. During this last period of my life, I have cried so many tears. I thought I would never stop crying. While other times, I was afraid because I did not cry first thing in the morning or in the afternoon, but the evening and into the night I could not stop crying. There is no crystal ball that gives you the ability to determine if you are going to cry today or not.

Give yourself permission to cry and to use the tears as a journey to accept change. It is hard to make headway when the challenges of life have immobilized you. Sobbing does not make you weak, but it allows you to purge feelings of hurt, sadness, reluctance, unknown questions and anything else that you are experiencing. Crying is ultimately the mechanism that will help you see things in a new light and giving you a place in life to be free. Be still, cry and take steps to move forward.

# LESSON: 9

## GRIEF COMES AND GOES

This is such a true statement. There are triggers that make grief happen and times where you are feeling good and bad. It can be a song, a movie, the smell of perfume or cologne, the savory or sweet smell of food or a host of other things that make you remember details about your loved one.

Holidays, birthdays, and anniversaries remind you that grief is still present and that it can come and go all in the same moment. It comes in spurts. Take time to be in that moment.

# LESSON: 10

## GET PROFESSIONAL HELP

Seeking professional help is still somewhat taboo in the certain ethnic groups and church communities. Many people seek the help of their pastor or clergy member to get them through the death of a loved one. While others utilize the services of their employer's counseling program and some combine the services of both.

This can be very helpful. Whichever one a person considers or ultimately uses, take the time to research the services. Only you can make the decision of which is best for you, and your family. I personally found that both the religious aspect and individual counseling has been helpful to me. As a clinician, I advocate and am in favor of counseling because I believe in the value of therapy. Consider the pros and cons of therapy and the possible outcomes. Do not be afraid to get help for yourself with your healing.

# LESSON: 11

# THANK GOD FOR THE BLESSINGS

Blessings are gifts from God. Each day that you can receive one, remember that you are the receiver of the gift. Blessings can come in disguises all during this process. Although your loved one has departed, this does not mean that their life was not a blessing to you. Look at their life for all the things they have taught you, the things they shared with you and what you have shared with them. Remember the good times and allow yourself to be fully engaged in those moments. Blessings will continue to follow you even as you create and demand a new life.

# LESSON: 12

---

## CELEBRATE LIFE

When a loved one passes, it is hard sometimes to think about what life will be like without them. It is hard to move on and fathom what shall I do now that they are gone. In the countless experiences I have encountered with people who have lost loved ones, this question is probably the one that is the most asked and the least prepared to answer. How do you go on when you lose a spouse, a child or the breadwinner of your household? What do you do now that they are gone? What challenges will you face?

These questions are many that will continue to plague the loved one after the loss. One day at a time, one decision at a time and the support of family and friends can help to celebrate life. When you decide to celebrate life, believe that you can move on and make decisions that honor yourself and the memory of your loved one. Enlist the relationships that you have built along the way in order to support your new life. You will never be the same, but you will always be guided by the memories!

# BONUS LESSONS

# GRATITUDE

How do you have gratitude in the midst of a storm, when life is challenging and when you are still reeling and rocking from grief? How do you keeping moving and doing what is right, in what way do you show your gratitude for this experience?

You do this by pondering and thinking about the life that you have and how you lived your life with your beloved. It is a blessing to be able to spend time with people and to share in their lives. Each person that we meet comes into our lives for a reason, season or lifetime. We are challenged to embrace the lessons that we will learn and to continue to use those lessons in order to share them with others. In this journey we call life it is full of ups and down and so much in between.

So where do you find the gratitude? You find it in every thought, every memory, and every moment of laughter. This just makes for a wonderful reason to be happy and to think back to what was once a profound time in your life. I am grateful for what I have been given to experience. It was truly a gift and I will continue to embrace what I have learned along the way.

In the still moments of life, I am grateful for and have gratitude for the relationship that I was able to forge and the life experiences. This has taught me many lessons, but the biggest one of all is that love is waiting on you; you just have to be ready in order to receive it.

Take the gratefulness of the moment that you live and continue to seek opportunities to be grateful even in spite of some of life's circumstances. The journey that I am on now is not without the still longing of what I once had but now it is truly discovering the purpose within my pain. I am in a different headspace that I once was and this is one that I am cultivating while honoring life with and serving others. I am grateful for being able to share my experiences and to be very transparent about my journey.

# HOLIDAY PLAN A & B

The holidays are a time for celebration however when you lose someone near and dear to you, the realization that they are no longer here to celebrate still resonates with you and it makes you sad. How do you plan to get through the holidays? What is your game plan, do you have a Plan A or B? What is the one piece of advice that you can give to someone as they navigate the upcoming holiday season? How did you get through the holiday this year? For me I had to get my Plan A and B in place before the actual holiday came. I have to admit I was feeling very, very sad as the routine that I had been accustomed to was now forever changed. I am grateful to be in the space I was in because it allowed me to live and know my true reality at that very moment.

# JOURNAL TO HEALING

I turned to writing and journaling in order to help me process my feelings, my tears, and my unanswered questions. Journaling is healing and it is also cathartic. I began to write, write and write until I just could not stop writing. I began to really use what had been poured into me in order to help heal myself. I would sometimes just pull out my notebook and write even if it was only a few minutes a day. This would help me gather my thoughts and feeling for that moment. Some days the journal entry would be long and others days they were just a mere short few words. The process has helped me to see that I am vulnerable and yet responsible for what I write down. I can also track my growth. My journaling is an outward expression of my love that I am now continuing to honor by putting forward my best work to help others become bigger, better, faster and stronger in life.

Journaling has been one of the best pieces of advice given to me along my journey and it birthed my book! At times I would stare at a blank page of my journal and just cry. After I cried I would feel better and begin to write. Sometimes I would still need a bit more coaching and play with my words. I would start writing words on paper and then an idea would form!

I am sharing an exercise on my blog that I hope will help someone on today. Join me in filling in the blanks.

I remember when I:

_____

_____

_____

_____

_____

_____

_____

_____

If you were writing a story, what would your main character say to you to help you move forward on today?

_____

_____

_____

_____

_____

_____

_____

_____

# *Conversations with God*

## *The Devotional*

(Excerpts from my e-book)

# Loss of a Significant Other

*Give thanks in all circumstances; for this is the will of God in Christ Jesus for you.*
*1Thessalonians 5:18*

Losing a significant person in your life can be one of the most devastating things that one has to go through. You never get over it. You just learn to live without them. You try to remember the good times, but the bad times resurface as well. Even in the midst of the loss, you still want to know the reasons why. What could I have done to prevent this? Is there anything I could have done? How can I go on? These are the questions and conversations that you have with God about the outcome. Where do I begin to rebuild and how do I even consider love once you are gone? No one will ever replace you or be like you. I wonder if the reasons why will even be provided or explained. I continue to look to God for comfort and often still wonder why.

## *Prayer*

*Lord, help me to accept your will. Help me to understand the reasoning and trust your ways. I acknowledge and give full surrender to you. In your wonderful and magnificent name, Amen*

# Loss of a Broken Relationship

*The Lord is near to those who are discouraged; he saves those who have lost all hope.*
*Psalm 34:18*

It can be devastating when you lose a relationship. Why is this happening? What did I do? How can I fix this? What did I miss? These are some of the things that can be said when a person suffers the loss of the broken relationship. Relationships can expire for a variety of reasons such as death, moving away from home, attending college or starting a new beginning. Whatever the reasons are, things are based on information that we know and sometimes we do not. We can come up with a thousand questions as to why this happened and why things worked out the way they did, but just know that there was a reason for the breakup. It may be for the protection of the heart. It may because of illness. It may be because of tragedy or a host of other reasons. Remember you are being protected for a reason and trust God in His plan.

## *Prayer*

*Father, I really want to know why? What is it that I was being protected from? Thank you for protecting me when I want to know your reason. Allow me to take the information and reasons why in order to be a different and new creature in you. Amen.*

# Loss of a Child(ren)

**Lo, Children are an heritage of the Lord; and the fruit of the womb is his reward.**
**Psalm 127:3**

There is a saying that a parent should never experience the loss of a child. It seems in this day and age that, this is happening more and more often due to gun violence, accidental deaths, drug addictions and even incarceration. All of these things and many more can lead to losing a child(ren). It is never easy losing a child but there are certain things that are lost if this happens. The loss of security, the loss of a mothers touch, the loss of a listening ear and even the loss of not being able to touch your child is what happens when one loses that child.

## *Prayer*

*God bring comfort and peace to me as I remember my child.*
*Your name means peace, so I ask that you help me*
*experience it on today. In your precious name, I pray.*
*Amen.*

# SCRIPTURES ON GRIEF

## Psalm 34:18

The LORD is near to the brokenhearted and saves the crushed in spirit.

## Psalm 73:26

My flesh and my heart may fail, but God is the strength of my heart and my portion forever.

## Psalm 119:50

My comfort in my suffering is this: Your promise preserves my life.

## Matthew 5:4

"Blessed are those who mourn, for they shall be comforted.

## 2 Corinthians 1:3-4

Blessed be the God and Father of our Lord Jesus Christ, the Father of mercies and God of all comfort, who comforts us in all our affliction, so that we may be able to comfort those who are in any affliction, with the comfort with which we ourselves are comforted by God.

## Philippians 4:6-7

Do not be anxious about anything, but in every situation, by prayer and petition, with thanksgiving, present your requests to God. 7 And the peace of God, which transcends all understanding, will guard your hearts and your minds in Christ Jesus.

## 1 Peter 5:7
Casting all your care upon him; for he careth for you.


## Romans 5:13
May the God of hope fill you with all joy and peace as you trust in him, so that you may overflow with hope by the power of the Holy Spirit.

# AFFIRMATIONS FOR HEALING

Here are the affirmation that I have found that have served me well and continue to be an integral part of my daily mediation and routine.

- You are loved
- You are worthy
- My dear friend, never, never give up!
- Faith makes all things possible
- Be kind to yourself
- I am grateful for the experiences I have had
- I am remembering love
- I am open to healing
- Today I am open to possibilities
- I am successful and have a purpose in life

# Grief and Loss Resources

Grief.com(Grief.com)

GriefNet.org ( www.griefnet.org )

The National Center for Grieving Children and Families

(www.dougy.org)

Open to Hope (opentohope.com)

Center for Loss and Transition (www.centerforloss.com)

Hello Grief (Hellogrief.org)

GoodTherapy.org  (Goodtherapy.org)

Psychology Today(Psychologytoday.com)

OpenPathCollective (Openpathcollective.org)

Suicide Helpline (1-800-273-8255)

Grief Recovery after a Substance Passing (760-262-8612)

National Alliance for the Mentally Ill (1-800-950-NAMI)

National Institute of Mental Health (1-800-421-4211)

Rainbows (1-847-952-1774)

# Personal Reflections

_____

_____

_____

_____

_____

_____

_____

_____

_____

_____

_____

_____

_____

_____

## ABOUT THE AUTHOR

Cherie L. Barnes is a clinician, author, and speaker, child of God and founder of The Healing Group. Cherie is the author of Conversations with God: The Devotional. As an advocate of healing, Cherie uses her own experiences and others of grief and loss to tell stories that help individuals find meaning in life and support positive actions. Cherie has a master degree in Counseling, is a National Certified Counselor, and is a lifelong learner who studies at the University of Life. When she is not glued to her computer, she enjoys cooking, binge-watching the Food Network, writing, and volunteer work. She is currently working on a children's book on grief and loss and a book of poems.

For upcoming events and booking visit: CherieBarnesAuthor.com or join the free Facebook community, *The Healing Group*, where you will be inspired and find encouragement while healing from grief, loss, and trauma.

www.ingramcontent.com/pod-product-compliance
Lightning Source LLC
Chambersburg PA
CBHW070751050426
42449CB00010B/2422

* 9 7 8 1 9 4 8 8 2 9 0 1 4 *